Original title:
The Charm of Every Moment

Copyright © 2025 Creative Arts Management OÜ
All rights reserved.

Author: Zachary Prescott
ISBN HARDBACK: 978-1-80586-182-9
ISBN PAPERBACK: 978-1-80586-654-1

Traces of Bliss in Stillness

In the quiet, a cat takes a leap,
Chasing dust motes, a dance so deep.
A sock on the floor, a mystery throne,
Socks will unite, but one stays alone.

A coffee cup's smile, a tickle on lips,
Spills of laughter, and liquid sips.
A chair with a squeak, a hiccup before,
As friends share gossip, the room fills with roar.

Kaleidoscope of Present Joys

A jester stands tall in the crowd of the sane,
With banana peels plush, it's quite the game.
A pie in the face, laughter erupts,
And friendships are sealed with playful erupts.

A rainbow of snacks, a buffet so bright,
Eating too much, though the pants feel tight.
With each silly moment, joy starts to grow,
Like finding a dollar in winter's deep snow.

Threads of Serendipity

A squirrel with a hat and a mischievous grin,
Steals the last fry while we all laugh and spin.
Stumbling on laughter in an unexpected way,
We trip over joy like it's a game we all play.

A dance in the kitchen while dinner's on hold,
With spatulas waving, we're all feeling bold.
The chaos of joy, like a confetti storm,
In moments so silly, we find our warm.

Ode to Unseen Magic

A puddle reflects the silliness found,
Where kids leap with glee, slipping loudly around.
The sprinkle of rain, it rhymes with our cheer,
Like laughter in echoes, we hold it all dear.

An old joke resurfaces, dusted and neat,
As we spice it with giggles that make life sweet.
With each little moment, a snapshot we frame,
In the gallery of now, we're all part of the game.

Ephemeral Elegance

A rubber chicken on the floor,
Invites a laughter that we adore.
Slips and slides with graceful flair,
Wobbly dance in the summer air.

A cake that's leaning to the right,
Takes a tumble, what a sight!
Frosting flies and folks all laugh,
Our joyous mess — a tasty craft.

Captured Instants

A cat that jumps and misses high,
Crashes lands, it seems to fly.
With beats of paws, a silly sprint,
In slow-mo, time, the twinkles hint.

A toast to cheers that spill like rain,
With fizzy bursts, it's pure champagne.
We laugh it off with silly glee,
Our carefree spirits want to be free.

Dance of the Seconds

A clock that ticks with style and grace,
Turns our worries into a race.
Each tick-tock brings a zany cheer,
Time's a prankster, drawing near.

In goofy hats, we twirl about,
Spinning in joy, erasing doubt.
The seconds dance and whirl around,
In every chuckle, happiness found.

Twilight's Embrace

With fireflies wearing tiny hats,
Buzzing around, they tease our chats.
The shadows stretch as we do prance,
Awkward moves in a silly dance.

As night settles, we eat dessert,
The pie's a mess, oh, what a flirt!
Laughter echoes, twinkling skies,
In moments where each giggle flies.

Serenity in the Now

Coffee spills on my shirt,
The cat pounces, what a flirt.
Laughing at the toast that burnt,
Life's little joys, I'm sure they won't hurt.

A sock hides, a mystery lost,
I trip, but pay no real cost.
The world is silly, bright, and round,
In chaos, sweet delight is found.

A Symphony of Small Wonders

Birds sing loudly, off-key tunes,
A squirrel dances under the moons.
Ice cream drips down my chin with glee,
Oh, these sweet messes are just for me.

Sidewalk chalk paints dreams so bold,
Hot wheels racing, stories told.
Each tiny moment, a comic show,
Laughter bubbles, watch it grow.

Dappled Light on a Sidewalk

Sunlight dapples, shadows play,
A dog prances in a silly way.
Umbrella hats? Why not, I dare!
Life's bizarre, but I do not care.

Pigeon struts like it owns the street,
Children skip to a shuffling beat.
All the quirks carry me afar,
Moments sparkle like a shooting star.

Laughter Beneath the Surface

Bubbles rise in my fizzy drink,
Silly faces make me think.
From silly dances to goofy pranks,
Joy is free, let's give it thanks.

In a puddle, reflections of fun,
Dancing shadows, as day is done.
Life's light-hearted tricks, they tease,
Chasing smiles like a gentle breeze.

Unraveled Moments of Grace

A cat in a hat sits high on a chair,
Pondering life with a curious stare.
Spilled milk leads to a dance on the rug,
While socks fly away like they're part of a bug.

The toast did a flip, a marvelous sight,
Landing butter-side down, oh what a fright!
In laughter we flourish, in silliness thrive,
Each giggle we share keeps our dreams alive.

Palette of Precious Whispers

With crayons in hand, a masterpiece drawn,
A scribble that glows like a brightening dawn.
But the paper's a cat, it has other plans,
And suddenly it's just colored-up hands!

A cake in the oven, it rises so grand,
'Til it leaps out of bounds, making quite a stand.
In chaos we find such whimsical glee,
As we savor each slice with joy, you and me.

Whispers of Time

Tick-tock goes the clock, it's time to be late,
Chasing lost keys, oh what a grand fate!
Coffee splashes high, it's a caffeinated thrill,
Life crackles with laughter, there's always a spill.

A squirrel steals my lunch, a mischievous thief,
While I ponder my snack with comic relief.
In every small incident, joy takes its stand,
A silly reminder, life's at our command.

Fleeting Glimmers

A bubble floats high, a fragile delight,
Until it pops loud, oh what a fright!
Sunshine's a prankster, it tickles the ground,
As we chase rolling shadows that dance all around.

A dog in a tutu twirls with such grace,
Spinning in circles, embracing the space.
With laughter our treasures, we collect every grin,
In each fleeting moment, the fun's just begin.

Moments in Bloom

In a garden of giggles, we dance around,
As bees buzz with laughter, not making a sound.
A tulip trips over its own pretty shoelace,
While daisies play tag in a polka-dot race.

Sunflowers wink under the bright summer sky,
As snails wear their shells like a suit and a tie.
We laugh at the clouds, who forgot how to float,
While kittens perform their acrobat routine, quite remote.

Elegy of the Present

In this grand comedy, life takes a bow,
As we trip over shoelaces, no way to disavow.
A toast to the moments made awkward with grace,
Like penguins who waddle in a formal embrace.

Time sings a ditty of misplaced socks,
While frogs in top hats tap dance on rocks.
The clock ticks in laughter, not ticking away,
As we juggle our worries like it's a child's play.

Captivated by Now

Here's to the giggles, the pratfalls, the slaps,
To dogs in hot pursuit of their owners' mishaps.
A squirrel steals lunch with a cheeky little grin,
While ducks in a row conga, let the fun begin.

The toaster pops up like a jack-in-the-box,
As I dance in the kitchen with mismatched socks.
Each hiccup a moment, with joy interceded,
In a casserole of laughter, we're thoroughly seeded.

Time's Gilded Pages

On yellowed parchment, we write with our sighs,
They curl like the smoke from a pizza surprise.
Photographs giggle as they capture our glee,
While friends start a riot with a slice of brie.

The clock wears a bowtie, looking quite spry,
As we ponder if moose ever learn how to fly.
Each tick is a chuckle, each tock a delight,
In the laughter of seconds, we take flight.

Threads of Time

Tick-tock goes the clock,
As I juggle socks.
I spill my morning brew,
And wear it like a shoe.

My cat has taken flight,
Chasing shadows at night.
My watch just lost its hand,
Now it's part of the band.

The dog's doing ballet,
In his own special way.
He leaps toward a treat,
Ends up dancing on his feet.

Running late is an art,
With breakfast on my shirt.
But I laugh through the chase,
On this wild, silly race.

Heartbeats in Harmony

Two left feet and a dance,
Oh, what a funny chance!
I trip on my own toes,
But the laughter just grows.

The neighbors all complain,
My karaoke's insane.
Yet I'm belting out tunes,
Under the watching moon.

My heart beats out a song,
In a rhythm that's wrong.
Stumbling through the day,
Still, I find a way to play.

Cupcakes fall from the sky,
And I won't even cry.
With each sprinkle and laugh,
I'm the jester on my path.

A Canvas of Today

With crayons I create,
A masterpiece of fate.
But somehow, on the floor,
There's more paint than before.

The cat decided to help,
With a splash and a yelp.
Now the walls are a sight,
Of green, pink, and bright white.

I paint my friend's big nose,
Then I dress it with prose.
This canvas tells our tale,
With giggles that prevail.

Every splotch and each line,
Makes this moment divine.
Who knew art could be fun,
When it's done on the run?

Fragments of Forever

Collecting moments one by one,
Each giggle shines like the sun.
With every slip and every fall,
We find the joy in it all.

I lost my shoe today,
As it flew far away.
Chasing it down the street,
Tripping over my own feet.

The ice cream made a splash,
As I tried to make it fast.
With sticky hands I shout,
"This is what life's about!"

In a whirlwind of delight,
We spin into the night.
Each laugh, a shining star,
In this silly memoir.

Now and Always

Life's a trip, with snacks galore,
We laugh so loud, hearts want more.
Dancing in socks, we glide and slip,
Chasing our dreams, on a banana peel trip.

Jellybeans rain, from the sky so high,
We catch them all, oh me, oh my!
With each silly giggle, we paint the air,
Time's a jester, with tricks to share.

Iridescent Echoes

Tickle the clock, it giggles back,
A tick-tock dance, on a crooked track.
We wear mismatched socks and silly hats,
In this world, we're all acrobats!

Lollipop dreams and popcorn streams,
Frogs in tuxedos, bursting at the seams.
With laughter as the melody, we sway,
In this crazy waltz, we find our way.

Moments like Echoes

A bubble pops, laughter's the sound,
We race with shadows, joy unbound.
From sips of lemonade, to wild charades,
Unfolding fun, in sunshine cascades.

Turning mundane into grand affairs,
With goofy goggles and wild stares.
Each moment a spark, in our zany quest,
Together we laugh, we are truly blessed.

Vignettes of Time

A cat in a hat, oh what a sight,
We laugh till we cry, in pure delight.
Spinning like tops, with tea and cakes,
Chasing the giggles, wherever it takes.

With ice cream drips, and wobbly chairs,
Life's a circus, with all its flares.
In every oddity, we find our tune,
Under the gaze of a chuckling moon.

Symphony of Seconds

Tick-tock goes the clock,
A dance that makes us laugh.
Each second plays a tune,
It's time for a silly gaffe.

Jellybeans on the floor,
A slip, a tumble, whoops!
We giggle through the fall,
In life's playful loops.

Doodles on the napkin,
With crayons, nothing's bland.
We sketch our silly dreams,
In a colorful, fun land.

Whispers of a cat's purr,
And hiccups from the pup.
In each moment we embrace,
We relish, we erupt!

Treasure of Tides

Wave after wave of joy,
Seagulls stealing our chips.
Sandcastle peaks tumble,
As laughter sloshes and slips.

Treasure hunters we are,
With spoons and beachy flair.
Digging for lost giggles,
With sandbags we declare.

Crabs in a funky dance,
Waving claws like a cheer.
We mimic their antics,
And cause the whole beach to leer.

As the tide rolls on in,
And the sun starts to fade,
We pack up our treasures,
With memories made.

Flickers of Fate

A twinkling star above,
Debating pizza's allure.
With every slice a wish,
Who knew cheese can obscure?

Butterflies in the breeze,
They flutter, a comic feat.
In their quest for sweet blooms,
They forget about their feet.

Dancing under street lights,
With moves that can't be caught.
Each step is a misstep,
But we're laughing, why not?

When fortune takes a fall,
Like a clumsy friend's blunder,
We rise, twirl in delight,
With joy that breaks asunder.

Daydreams Unraveled

In a world made of marshmallows,
Floating on giggles and cheer.
We bounce on clouds of laughter,
As the sun tickles our ear.

Wild hats on our heads,
With fruit loops as our crowns.
We prance through silly fields,
In laughter, never frowns.

As the clock strikes giggle-o'clock,
We dive into playful schemes.
Building castles of candy,
Playing hopscotch on our dreams.

With every moment we savor,
In this whimsical parade,
We chase the joy that's fleeting,
Leaving memories that won't fade.

Serendipity's Kiss

I tripped on my shoelace, what a sight,
My coffee flew up, oh what a flight!
Laughter erupted, much to my glee,
Each stumble a dance, the world's not so free.

A bird stole my sandwich right off my plate,
I yelled 'Hey you!'—what a twist of fate!
In every mishap, a giggle I find,
A life full of folly, oh never so blind.

Splendor in the Strands

My hair's a wild mess, a glorious sight,
Caught on a doorknob, oh what a fright!
I laugh with the mirror, who needs a hairdo?
Daily adventures, each twist feels brand new.

Fluffy pancakes landed right on my head,
Thought I was dreaming, was surely misled!
With syrupy giggles, I dance in my room,
Embracing the chaos, no hint of gloom.

Threads of Illusion

I wore mismatched socks to a fancy event,
A fashion statement? Or just ill-spent?
A friend rolled her eyes, but I just couldn't care,
Every laugh shared, a magical air.

My cat thought my tie was a great new toy,
While I drank my drink, he caused such a joy!
In the realm of the strange, I happily drift,
Life's little quirks are an infinite gift.

Capturing the Now

I took a fine photo, but got my own face,
Captured the moment, in total disgrace!
My friends laughed so hard, I joined in the fun,
Each silly snapshot, a victory won.

Tickling my thoughts, the clock hits a stand,
The dog chased a squirrel, oh what a plan!
I freeze every giggle, each silly delight,
Life's fleeting snapshots bring boundless respite.

Reflections in Silence

In the quiet, a sneeze breaks the night,
Fish talk back to me, what a sight!
A chair squeaks, laughter in disguise,
Even shadows wear comical ties.

Whiskers twitch on the old cat's face,
He blinks like he's found a new place.
The clock ticks loudly, every tick a jest,
Time really knows how to be a pest.

A spoon does a jig on the table's end,
Coffee spills, oh what a friend!
I mean to sip, I meant to think,
But giggles arise from the clink of the drink.

As silence stirs with each silly thing,
Joy in whispers, a pet can sing.
Laughing, I dance with my random thoughts,
In this quiet chaos, happiness is caught.

Lanterns of Light

Balloons float by, chasing the breeze,
One popped loudly, oh how it frees!
Little giggles escape through the night,
Lanterns flicker, what a funny sight.

A squirrel steals snacks from a picnic spread,
Didn't invite him, yet he boldly fed!
Laughter echoes in the moon's embrace,
As I chase him, we both set pace.

Ghosts of laughter fill the warm air,
I trip on a branch—oops, what a scare!
The lanterns twinkle like stars gone mad,
Even the moon chuckles, a bit too glad.

In this carnival of shimmering beams,
Reality blends with animated dreams.
Each moment beckons to dance and sway,
With the lanterns glowing, I'll laugh away.

Unfolding Horizons

With each sunrise, a breakfast dare,
Spilled juice stains on a crumpled chair.
The toast jumps up, just like my heart,
A bird joins in, it's an awkward art.

Clouds parade in bizarre procession,
One looks like a cat, it's a fine obsession!
The sun winks down, a playful tease,
Suggesting we dance among the trees.

As colors bloom in the brightening sky,
Grass tickles my toes, oh me, oh my!
With each unpleasant sneeze that I make,
Maybe nature has jokes for my sake.

Horizons yawning, open like fans,
I prance around in my mismatched pants.
Funny moments sail with the breeze,
In this unfolding, I find my ease.

Remnants of Radiance

At dusk, the world wears a comical grin,
Fireflies glow like they're in a spin.
The moon's bright laugh breaks the day's sigh,
As I chase my hat that dares to fly.

Each shadow dances, a jester's parade,
Making friends with the serenade.
Old shoes squeak in a rhythm so loud,
I'm the star of an imaginary crowd.

Waves of laughter rise with the tide,
Seagulls squawk as if to chide.
Sunset splashes colors, vivid and bright,
Remnants remain, what a sight!

In moments fleeting, silliness stays,
Radiance speaks in the weirdest ways.
With a chuckle, I gather each beam,
In this light-hearted life, I dare to dream.

Echoes in the Breeze

A squirrel danced across the lane,
Chasing shadows, bold and vain.
It slipped and fell, gave a shout,
While onlookers all laughed about.

A pigeon strutted, puffed up wide,
Claiming glory with each small stride.
But when it slipped on a puddle's sheen,
It flapped its wings; oh, what a scene!

The breeze tickled a toddler's nose,
As giggles burst like sudden prose.
With one big stomp, a splash was made,
And laughter echoed—a grand charade!

Yet every chuckle waltzed away,
Like dandelion seeds at play.
In fleeting moments, joy did hum,
While life took pause; here comes the fun!

Luminous Visions

In a diner, fries flew through the air,
While ketchup bottles get a scare.
A burger slid like a racing car,
Smiles erupted; a funny bazaar!

The waiter juggled plates with flair,
But one slipped off—oh dear, beware!
It landed right in a milkshake's plop,
And everyone laughed; they couldn't stop!

The neon lights flickered on and off,
A cat sneezed; we all had to scoff.
It ran in circles, a furry fuzz,
A matching dance of joyous buzz!

Though moments spark like fireworks there,
The laughter we shared, we all could wear.
A tapestry of light and jest,
In every bite, we found our best!

A Tapestry of Whispers

In the park, a dog found a shoe,
It pranced like royalty—who knew?
With each step, it made a fuss,
Pretending it was famous, just like us!

Two kids played bow and arrow aim,
But ended up in laughter's game.
The arrows missed—a bee was struck,
And both took off; oh, what bad luck!

A couple picnicked, hoping for peace,
But ants came marching, seeking their feast.
Between bites, they swatted and swore,
While giggling still, they wanted no more!

In whispers soft, secrets unfurl,
Amidst madcap moments, laughter whirls.
Each burst of joy like blooms in spring,
A dance of delight that life will bring!

Strokes of Splendor

A painter spilled his purples wide,
Confetti colors caught the tide.
His canvas laughed; he scratched his head,
As it turned into a lovely spread!

An artist giggled, shirt splashed bright,
Swirling colors, a true delight.
With each stroke, a story flowed,
His palette danced; inspiration glowed!

A cat sneezed on a fresh brush stroke,
Creating art with a clever joke.
The painter laughed, hands covered in paint,
A masterpiece formed, a life so quaint!

Through brush and laughter, worlds collide,
In strokes of splendor, let joy abide.
Each moment ticked, a vibrant cheer,
As colors swirled, we knew joy was near!

Radiance of the Here

Life's a dance, a silly jig,
We trip and laugh, we swerve too big.
A toast to crumbs on our toast,
And socks that don't match—what do I boast?

A cat that sings, a dog that prances,
We slip on dreams, take wild chances.
Oh, the joy of a banana peel!
A fruity slip, quite the comedic deal!

With light bulbs buzzing, we light our way,
Turning each fumble into a play.
Come, let's gather all the quirks,
And make a show with our silly works.

So take a moment, let laughter ignite,
In the quirkiest day, there's pure delight.
For each stumble is a tale to tell,
In the radiance of here, we smile so well.

Tapestry of Time

Tick-tock, tick-tock, the watch's a clown,
It spins and twirls, wants to paint the town.
A coffee spill, a noodle fight,
In this wacky weave, everything's right!

The calendar sings with silly notes,
Reminding us of laundry, and that goat that floats.
Oh, pants on the attic, socks by the sea,
Each thread of chaos is just wild glee.

We tie our shoelaces with spaghetti strands,
Juggling emotions with our quirky hands.
Memory dances, quite out of sync,
We laugh till the tears spill—oh, what do we think?

In the patchwork of laughs, we stitch and we sway,
With threads of joy making folly play.
Each moment a fiber in the cosmic rhyme,
Spinning the tapestry all through time.

Every Breath a Wonder

Inhale a giggle, exhale a grin,
Count the hiccups, where do we begin?
With each little puff, we're tickled pink,
As marshmallows float by; what do you think?

A sneeze that sounds like a BRR-RING!
An epic tale of the oddest bling.
The phone that buzzes like it's in a race,
Spilling the tea on my neighbor's face!

Breath of a duck in a baseball cap,
Every chuckle wrapped in a little nap.
And when we stumble over our feet,
Each misstep's a win—you gotta admit!

So toast to the breath, each moment, a gem,
In the wheeze of life, let's never condemn.
For wonder resides in the strangest sights,
With laughter as our guide, soaring new heights.

Timeless Whispers

Whispers in the wind make quite the jest,
They tickle our ears—come laugh with zest!
A squirrel in glasses reads a book,
In this merry moment, let's take a look!

Each tick of the clock brings giggles too,
With banter of crickets, and a frog or two.
They croak our secrets, oh what a thrill,
In every breeze, there's laughter to spill!

So skip through a puddle, dance on a shard,
Embrace the absurd, it's never too hard.
For time is but whispers, but let's keep it loud,
With chuckles and joy, let's laugh out proud.

In timeless echoes, what stories unfold,
With each sparkle of laughter, the memories hold.
So cherish the fun before it goes far,
In the whispers of now, we are the stars.

Portraits of Pulses

In the fridge, a pickle grins,
Winks at me with sour sins.
I laugh at its cheeky stare,
Best friends in our fridge affair.

A cat leaps like it stole a dance,
Yet trips in a silly prance.
Her indignation, a sight to see,
Spilling laughter in our spree.

A squirrel swipes my sandwich quick,
With a dash and a comical flick.
Nature's heist, what a display,
Each moment, a giggling play!

Life's simple joys, we can't ignore,
From the pickle's grin to the cat's snore.
Every beat, a laugh or cheer,
Collecting chuckles through the year.

Luminous Fleeting

A firefly's glow, a comic show,
Buzzing near, then off it will go.
I chase each blink with great delight,
Tripping over shadows in the night.

The toast pops up, a sudden jump,
Like it's a toast to the morning's thump.
Spilled coffee, a caffeinated art,
Each mishap, a giggle to start.

The dog in a sweater, oh so proud,
Struts like royalty, yells out loud.
Yet with one leap, it's off the floor,
Finding a pillow to snore and roar.

Every fleeting flicker feels so bright,
Turning blunders into sheer delight.
Life's little quirks, a silly parade,
In this whimsical escapade.

Embrace of the Instant

An ice cream cone, a tower tall,
Toppling over with a comedic sprawl.
Laughter erupts at that gooey scene,
Moments sticky, yet oh-so-keen.

A jogger trips on a playful breeze,
Flutters like leaves, trying to appease.
His flailing arms, a wild charade,
Painting joy in this sunny glade.

A squirrel's chatter, absurdly loud,
Complains about life in its fluffy shroud.
I nod along, a silly debate,
As if we're discussing our fate.

Each instant filled with unexpected glee,
Finding laughter in life's decree.
From melting treats to nature's jest,
Moments like these are simply the best.

The Poetry of Now

The cat on the window, contemplating life,
With its dramatic flair and plastic knife.
Each pounce a stanza, each stretch a rhyme,
Living in a world that's quickly sublime.

A toddler's dance, pure chaos in fun,
Spinning around like a mini-sun.
With every twirl, a giggle cascades,
Turning the living room into parades.

A sandwich named 'leftover surprise',
Half a pickle and two stale fries.
Though odd on the plate, it tastes like bliss,
Promising laughter in every bite's kiss.

In each quirky detail, joy does endow,
The verses of laughter in the poetry of now.
Embracing each laugh in a lighthearted bow,
Finding the wonder in life's sweet wow.

Luminous Flickers of Today

In the kitchen, I drop my toast,
Landing butter-side up, what a boast!
The cat jumps high, it's quite the show,
As I laugh alone, with breakfast in tow.

The coffee spills as I dance a jig,
In my silly socks, I feel quite big.
A sock puppet talks; I nod and grin,
Life's silly moments, where do I begin?

A bird outside chirps a funny tune,
Twirling a feather like a tiny balloon.
I trip on my shoelace, oh what a sight,
Laughter erupts, turning wrong into right.

The phone rings loud, it's my friend's pet,
A voice so ridiculous, I can't forget.
We share silly jokes 'til the sun goes down,
These luminous flickers, they never drown.

Secret Lives of Fleeting Instants

A blueberry falls, and rolls away,
Chasing it down, I'm in a play.
It dodges my grasp with a cheeky grin,
Rolling under the fridge, it's won again!

Invisible socks have an evening spree,
They dance with glee, just not with me.
As I search for match pairs, they laugh in shame,
Jokingly leading me back to the game.

The clock ticks slowly on this grand day,
Every second winks like it wants to play.
I take a step and stumble on air,
Even gravity seems to be in despair!

Digesting these moments, like a tasty treat,
Crumbs of laughter make life feel sweet.
In the mix of chaos, joy has its way,
These fleeting instants never decay.

Embracing Simple Marvels

A dandelion puff, floating with grace,
Kids chase it down, in a wild race.
They laugh and tumble, oh what a sight,
These simple marvels, oh pure delight!

A snail takes its time, strikes a pose,
Looking so proud as it slowly goes.
I cheer it on, what a grand pace,
Who knew that slow could win the race?

The bees make a buzz, trying their best,
Hoping for nectar, they fail the rest.
With pollen on noses, they buzz and bounce,
I can't help but chuckle, oh what a flounce!

Rain drops dance like a spastic crew,
As puddles reflect a topsy-turvy view.
In these small wonders, we find our fun,
Embracing simplicity until day is done.

Starlit Smiles Beneath the Mundane

Laundry piles high, socks in disarray,
I ponder their mission—are they here to play?
Each shriek of the dryer, a crisp little joke,
I giggle and wrestle, what a wild folk!

An awkward dance in the grocery lane,
Dodging carts like I'm playing a game.
The cereal aisle, a colorful spree,
I grab a box shaped like a bumblebee!

Beneath the desk, a rogue crumb I find,
I salute its bravery, it's one of a kind.
A dust bunny giggles, spinning 'round tight,
It claims the title of MVP tonight!

Life beneath stars with smiles so wide,
In each silly moment, there's joy to ride.
With laughter we twist, and spin in a trance,
These starlit smiles spark the most fun dance.

Time's Handprint

Tick-tock, the clock's a tease,
Wearing socks with quirky cheese.
Running late, I'll trip and fall,
Laughing echoes down the hall.

Each sip of tea's a tiny dance,
Caught in laughter, lost in glance.
Cake on face, a messy show,
Who knew cake could steal the glow?

Hiccups sound like giggles loud,
While trying hard to make a crowd.
Chasing after moments fleet,
We trip on laughs beneath our feet.

Snail mail dreams and paper planes,
A serenade of silly gains.
Life's a flick, a wobbly ride,
With chuckles bouncing, high and wide.

Fleeting Rhythms

Dancing socks on polished floors,
Like rubber chickens, oh, the roars!
Spinning round, we lose our shoes,
While laughter fills the air like blues.

Potato chips and funny hats,
Whispering secrets to the cats.
Every lease upon a giggle,
Teases time to twist and wiggle.

Ice cream drips and sticky hands,
Mapping joy through sugar strands.
Counting seconds on the run,
Can't stop smiling, just too fun!

Tickle fights and silly pranks,
Living life like we're in flanks.
Each little hiccup, whisper low,
Makes every instant steal the show.

Dappled in Delight

Sunshine peeks through window blinds,
Dancing feet with playful minds.
Juggling clouds like cotton candy,
Every giggle feels quite dandy.

Bubble gum and silly screams,
Leaping high on wobbly beams.
Chasing laughter, can't be caught,
Moments burst like popcorn, hot!

Dripping colors, paints a scene,
Sketching smiles, lives evergreen.
Whirling round on merry-go,
In this moment, joy we sow.

Lollipops and wiggly tails,
Life's a game of tipsy trails.
Every heartbeat's chanting sweet,
Wrapped in laughter, oh, what a treat!

Reflections of Rapture

Hiccups dance like tiny bugs,
In moments wrapped in goofy hugs.
Chasing shadows that just won't stay,
Silly faces brightening gray.

Belly laughs throughout the night,
With pillows flying in delight.
Every misstep, a brand new route,
With rubber ducks, we twirl about!

Coffee spills and frantic spills,
Time is nimble, full of thrills.
Sipping sunshine, feeling bright,
In the chaos, find our light.

Every pause, a chuckling sigh,
Moments fluttering like a fly.
Life's a jester, what a show,
Together in this funny flow.

A Symphony of Now

The clock says it's time for a snack,
But I'm lost in a meme, that I just can't hack.
My coffee's gone cold, like my last bad joke,
Yet I'll sip and I'll smile, as my phone starts to poke.

Birds tweet like they know my entire life story,
While I forget my socks, in a dance of pure glory.
I trip on a word, laughter fills the air,
Each stumble a note in my offbeat affair.

Every glance at the sky's a missed opportunity,
Like my attempts at adulting, void of continuity.
Yet here's where I stand, in absurdity's light,
Cracking up at the mundane, feeling so right.

So let's waltz through today, with a wiggle and twist,
Caught in the chaos, we simply can't resist.
With silly hats on, let's make our own score,
In this symphony of now, we'll forever explore.

Starlit Memories

Underneath the stars, I lost my last shoe,
While friends laugh and point, like they always do.
I swear it was here, stuck in the grass,
But maybe it fled... or just saw my dance class.

With marshmallows roasting, I start to debate,
If my s'mores are better, or just fashionably late.
Each sticky bite takes me back in time,
To that one awkward date, and my failed pick-up line.

Flashbacks of laughter, like fireflies they gleam,
Reminding me now, of just how to dream.
Yet every soft glow has a twist of the plot,
Like how I keep misplacing the things that I've got.

So let's keep on rolling, under this bright night,
With stories that sparkle, and moods that excite.
In the starlit glow, we'll embrace all we find,
As memories twinkle, and giggles unwind.

Hues of Transience

A rainbow of moments, bright paint on a wall,
But who dropped the bucket? It's splashed on us all!
With colors a-mix, and laughter awoke,
Just like my lunch, which I forgot to stoke.

Time flickers by like a cartoon on screen,
Where I trip on my words, and act so obscene.
Each brushstroke of life, has a quirk or a twist,
Like trying to dance, with a partner named Mist.

The fleeting hues blend, sometimes awkwardly so,
Like my outfit today — is it high fashion, or no?
Yet out in the chaos, I find such sweet zest,
In this canvas of moments, I'm truly the best.

So let's splash the world with our "oops" and our "whoa!",
Add a dash of confetti and allow it to flow.
In the art of today, we're the painters in play,
With hues of transience, let's color our way.

Secrets in Stillness

In the quiet of now, my sock starts to wiggle,
Is it trying to dance, or just caught in a squiggle?
There's wisdom in silence, or so the books say,
But that doesn't explain why I just lost my way.

The cat's plotting schemes, on a pile of old clothes,
While I sip from a mug, only I seem to know.
Each sip is a secret, a giggle in disguise,
Like waking up early to see if I'm wise.

Moments sit still, like a statue gone rogue,
Taunting me softly as I start to fog.
With each quiet pause, I'm refilling my cup,
Spilling stories and giggles, enough to erupt!

So let's savor the stillness, with laughs that abound,
Juggling our thoughts, making silence profound.
In the secrets we keep, let's find joy and cheer,
For life's little quirks bring us always so near.

Whispers in Passing Time

The clock ticks, a sly little prank,
Each second slips by with a giddy swank.
We chase our tails like puppies at play,
While time just giggles and runs away.

A toast to the moments we nearly forgot,
Like when I mistook soup for a pot!
Time waves goodbye with its cheeky grin,
As we stumble awkwardly and still try to win.

The bus stop's a stage for our wild dance,
Where strangers throw looks as if in a trance.
We laugh at our clumsiness, swat at the flies,
In a world where the absurd is a grand prize.

So let's relish the madness, embrace the spree,
With coffee spilled boldly on your new tee!
In each silly moment, a gem, can't you see?
These quirks of existence set our spirits free.

Fleeting Glimmers of Now

Life's a parade that's forever on speed,
With flowers that giggle and dance in the breeze.
We juggle our worries like clowns at the fair,
Each slip of the hand gives us room for a rare.

A wink from the universe, quick as a flash,
We stumble on laughter, like pies when they crash.
Who knew that a sneeze could be so sublime?
In this circus of chaos, we jest to defy time.

Those fleeting moments, where oddities bloom,
Like the cat that steals socks to keep in its room.
We laugh with abandon, ignore the calls home,
In this mad little world, oh how we do roam!

So here's to the quirks and the giggles that fly,
To the silly little things that make you ask why!
Let's trip over blessings and waltz with delight,
In this game of tomfoolery, we shine oh so bright.

Captured in a Heartbeat

A heartbeat's a wink, oh, how time can tease,
With moments that bubble like warm fondue cheese.
Like tripping on rainbows or juggling foam,
Who knew that our laughter could feel like a home?

Caught in the flicker of a firefly's blink,
We dance on the edge of a soft baby wink.
The world's a funhouse, each mirror a jest,
As we pirouette through a carnival quest.

Puddles reflect all the giggles we weave,
As we hop like kangaroos, intent to deceive.
A slip on a banana peel, oh what a jest,
We chuckle at mishaps, no need for a rest.

So toast to the wonder and all it bestows,
To the whims of the heart where the silliness flows.
In every heartbeat, a treasure we find,
A joyous connection that leaves us entwined.

Dances of Delight

In the dance of the day, we spin and we sway,
With hiccups of laughter that lighten the gray.
A misstep on purpose, a twirl that goes wrong,
Yet somehow we end up waltzing along.

The sun plays peek-a-boo, all warm and bright,
As shadows shimmy and join in the light.
We chase butterflies, arms wide in the air,
With giggles that soar as if without care.

A windy day turns our hats inside out,
We lose our cool but we never lose clout.
The world's a delight, a playful charade,
In whimsical moments, true joy is displayed.

So here's to the dances that life puts on show,
With every laugh shared, our spirits will grow.
In this whimsical waltz, together we'll glide,
With a grin and a giggle, let's enjoy the ride!

Echoes of the Present

Time is a jester, playing tricks,
Wearing mismatched socks and odd-patterned bricks.
We chase after minutes, they giggle and flee,
Like rabbits on roller skates—what a sight to see!

Each tick of the clock a sneaky little tease,
It knows all our secrets, even our sneeze.
We dance with our calendars, twirl with our plans,
But the universe laughs with its cosmic hands.

Life is a tapestry, woven quite tight,
With threads made of laughter and strange bits of light.
We wear goofy grins, with pie on our hats,
While riding the waves on our silly old mats.

So sip on that coffee, take life as it comes,
Embrace all the quirks, and dance like dumb chums.
When moments conspire to tease us just right,
We'll jump on the silliness—what a delight!

Celestial Caresses

Stars wink at us, with mischievous glee,
While comets join in for a grand jamboree.
We wave to the moon with our best cheesy grins,
As the universe chuckles, it knows all our sins.

Oh, Mercury, stop with your swift little pranks,
Messing with plans, and all those sweet flanks.
The night sky's a circus, a carnival bright,
Where wishes go giggling, taking their flight.

Planetary dance-offs under soft glowing light,
Mars just can't keep still, what a silly sight!
We ride shooting stars, like they're flinging pies,
With laughter echoing high in the skies.

So grab your telescope, let's watch the fun show,
Where black holes turn coffee into fizzy old dough.
Life's silly adventure is just a brief ride,
With cosmic confetti and joy as our guide!

Sunlit Reveries

Sunbeams bounce around, like children at play,
They giggle and chatter, diving into the day.
We wear silly hats, oh what a parade,
As flowers join in with their colorful charade.

The breeze teases softly, tickling our nose,
While clouds peek through branches, like secretive prose.

We skip with the shadows, embracing the light,
Each moment's a chance to dance with delight.

Picnics with ants, our unexpected guests,
Stealing crumbs from our sandwiches, such little pests!
We laugh as we swat them, and shine like the sun,
In this vibrant adventure, we're each having fun.

So raise up your voices, let echoes resound,
In this merry whirl where joy knows no bound.
Together we frolic, like leaves in a breeze,
Creating sweet memories, fantastical tease!

Moments Like Dew

Droplets of time hang on morning's soft breath,
Each winks with a sparkle, swaying with zest.
They dance on the petals, in tiny ballet,
As critters start buzzing, a humorous play.

Butterflies giggle, dodging right and left,
Sipping on nectar, they plan their big heist.
The flowers all chuckle, "Get in line, my friend!"
In this world of mischief, there's joy without end.

Moments like dew sparkle, then melt in the sun,
Quick as a hiccup, they vanish, then run.
Yet every sweet raindrop brings new laughter forth,
Each instant a treasure, a priceless worth.

So let's dance through the gardens, skip over the grass,
Where life's a surprise, and each moment's a class.
We'll giggle and play like kids on the go,
Embracing the joy, letting good vibes flow!

Elysian Foreshadows

In the garden of mischief, we play,
Dancing on daisies, in a silly ballet.
A bee with a bowtie, buzzing a tune,
While a cat shares gossip with a cartooned raccoon.

The sun throws a wink, slipping into green,
Toasts to the flowers, a vibrant cuisine.
Laughter bursts forth like a fizzy pop,
As frogs in tuxedos do their best hop.

A picnic of giggles beneath a grand tree,
Where squirrels masquerade as guests, you see.
The ants hold a party, it's quite the affair,
With crumbs of delight scattered everywhere.

As shadows grow longer, the fun never ends,
Throwing confetti, it's what nature sends.
In this whimsical world, absurd yet refined,
The joy of the moment, always aligned.

Transitions in Time

Tick-tock says the clock, a jester in gear,
As seconds slip by, in a comic cheer.
A turtle in sunglasses, strutting so slow,
While rabbits on rollerblades steal the show.

A briefcase of giggles, the day's busy plan,
Where every small mishap is part of the ban.
The sun takes a bow, it's getting quite late,
But starlight's in line for a whimsical fate.

In the whispers of dusk, fireflies conspire,
To light up the night, like a sparkly choir.
They dance and they twinkle, a wild parade,
As shadows play tricks in the cool evening shade.

The moon, ever teasing, peeks from behind,
With a wink and a smile, it's perfectly timed.
Laughter lingers gently, over hills it roams,
In this circus of moments, we find our homes.

Serene Suspensions

A hammock in laughter, where giggles reside,
With popcorn-shaped clouds on a light summer tide.
The weather is silly, with sprinkles of joy,
As rabbits launch rockets, oh what a ploy!

Butterflies twirl in their silly ballet,
While mischievous breezes refuse to obey.
Each tickle of wind brings a grin to the face,
As ducks in tuxedos join this sweet race.

Moments sit still, like a cat in the sun,
Where every shy whisper becomes part of fun.
Giggles of children echo near and far,
As ice cream drips down from a bright candy jar.

Under starlit giggles, we spin and we sway,
Mapping the moments, come what may.
Life's laughter, a treasure, we share with our friends,
In this wacky adventure, the fun never ends!

Euphoria in the Everyday

A cat on a roof, balancing like a pro,
Chasing its tail, putting on quite a show.
Coffee spills over, like a tiny fountain,
Lamp posts are watching, I swear they are counting.

Birds chirp in rhythm, a clumsy ballet,
Dancing on branches, in their own quirky way.
A squirrel with a nut, plotting its great heist,
Wonders if the world is just one big slice of pie.

Rain boots in puddles, splashing with glee,
Ducks in a row, singing in harmony.
A jogger trips over, laughing all the while,
Life's silly moments, oh, they make me smile!

A toddler with ice cream, the cone tilts and bends,
Sticky hands waving, making new friends.
Each giggle and snort wraps up the mundane,
In this wild circus, there's joy in the rain.

Joy Unveiled in Silence

In the quiet café, a spoon drops with a cling,
Barista is laughing, does a little fling.
A muffin's been caught in a sticky debate,
Should it be eaten, or tempt out its fate?

The clock takes a nap; it forgets to tick,
A warm breeze whispers, it's time for a trick.
Sweet pastry icons, each with their own story,
Make our mornings messy but oh-so-glory!

A sneeze in the corner sends laughter on high,
Someone nearby nearly takes to the sky.
Laughter erupts, it's a comedy scene,
As the muffins look on, oh, how they all preen!

In moments like these, the world feels alive,
With quirks and mishaps, oh how we thrive!
A sip of hot tea, a donut and cheer,
In silence so loud, camaraderie's here.

Tides of Tenderness

The dog on the beach is chasing his tail,
While seagulls swoop low, they plot and they sail.
Sand stuck on noses while kids build a fort,
Each wave a giggle, oh, what a report!

Flip-flops are flying, an unexpected breeze,
Someone yells loudly, "Oh please, don't tease!"
A picnic blanket says, "Share some with me!",
As sandwiches tumble, giggling by the sea.

Kites in the cloud, like dreams on a line,
A splash of cold water, an impromptu sign.
Laughter of children mixes sweetly with glee,
In this tide of hilarity, we dance by the sea.

As the sun dips low, the day fades away,
Each smile a treasure, that's here just to stay.
With joy in our hearts, we bundle and sway,
These tides transmit laughter, oh what a display!

Sunlit Stories Unfolding

Under the tall trees, a picnic unfolds,
Sandwiches waddle, their stories retold.
Giggling ants host a lively, loud dance,
As apples roll free, skipping in a trance.

Popsicles melting, what a sweet little mess,
Someone chokes softly on a sandwich, no less!
Lemonade splashes, a splash zone deemed fit,
For unleashing our giggles, and not losing it.

With kite tails twisting, a colorful might,
Trying to escape from an airborne fight.
A sunbeam slips through, glancing right in,
Casting shadows of laughter, where do we begin?

As the day drifts on, like a movie so bright,
We share silly moments, under soft moonlight.
Each tale a treasure, woven with cheer,
In sunlit embraces, the joys reappear.

Glances of Grace

A cat in a hat jumps high,
Chasing shadows that flit and fly.
My sock is missing, I can't complain,
It danced away in the morning rain.

A phone rings loud, it's a taco joint,
They've got my order ready, oh what a point!
But here I am, still in my jams,
Dancing in circles, avoiding the scams.

The teapot whistles, but I am not done,
Stirring sweet moments, it's all in good fun.
Spilled my coffee, it painted the floor,
A masterpiece now, who could ask for more?

Umbrellas flipping in a gusty breeze,
While birds squawk loudly in riotous tease.
I smile at the chaos, it's quite the show,
Life's goofy moments make time overflow.

Magic in the Mundane

A toast to toast, that golden slice,
With jelly glistening, it's oh so nice.
But there's a hair, a curl of my cat,
What a fine topping for breakfast chat!

The lawn gnome winks as I mow the grass,
In this mess of life, it's easy to pass.
A squirrel steals my sandwich while I sit,
Yet I laugh out loud, what a perfect fit!

My laundry's a whirl, colors collide,
A chaos of fabric I can't really hide.
Matching socks? Well, that's just for show,
Could be polka-dots dancing below!

Grocery shopping, a cart full of cheese,
Unruly children that run and tease.
A pickle in hand, I strike a pose,
Ah, life's little quirks, I simply chose.

Savoring the Sliver

A sliver of cake, a joyous delight,
But the fork's gone missing, oh what a plight!
So I use my fingers, frosting on nose,
With pastries and giggles, anything goes!

The sun beams down, making shadows dance,
While my dog prances, all in a trance.
Chasing his tail like a boss on a spree,
Such silly antics make me squeal with glee!

Inhale the perfume of a fresh-cut lawn,
While bees drop by for a sweet little yawn.
A picnic all set, but ants start to swarm,
With sandwiches gone, it's all part of the norm!

The doorbell rings, it's that friend I adore,
With jokes that tickle, we always want more.
In this cheerful chaos, we find our groove,
Savor each sliver, let laughter move!

Tides of the Present

Bubbles in the bath, I drift and play,
Toy boats sailing on a sudsy bay.
Rubber duck races, I cheer and shout,
In this tiny world, there's never a doubt.

The laundry spins, a whirlpool of cheer,
As socks lose their pairs, I shed a tear.
But what's this? A sock with a dancer's flair,
I giggle aloud, "Time has no care!"

Chasing after sunsets, wind in my hair,
With silly hats on, we haven't a care.
A dance-off with pigeons in the square,
Together we twirl, so blissfully rare!

Every tick of the clock brings laughter alive,
In ordinary moments, our spirits will thrive.
So join me in jest, let's embrace the jest,
In these tides of today, we truly are blessed!

Ephemeral Echoes

A wink from the sun, a shout from the breeze,
A squirrel in a suit, it's dancing with ease.
The puddles are mirrors, as I jump and I splatter,
The world's full of giggles, are you hearing the chatter?

A cloud drifts by, it's a fluffy wise guy,
It tells me to lighten, oh please, don't be shy.
I trip on my shoelace, oh what a delight,
The stars wink at me, embracing the night.

Moments are fleeting, like candy in air,
Watch out for seagulls, they're plotting, beware!
A tickle from daisies, they dance in a row,
I laugh at the clock, it's too fast, don't you know?

With each silly stumble, I learn to embrace,
The joy in the chaos, the thrill of the chase.
So here's to the laughter, the whimsy we find,
In every small moment, let's not leave behind.

Savoring the Seconds

Tick tock goes the clock, but I'm just too slow,
A sandwich just giggled, should I eat it or throw?
With each silly taste, I rumble and roar,
In a jungle of crumbs, who could ask for more?

A bike with no brakes, oh what a surprise,
It zooms past the park, beneath sunny skies.
The ice cream is melting, it's racing my tongue,
A sweet sticky chaos, let's get this done!

Every curvy pathway leads to fun where I go,
Playing hopscotch with puddles, just don't be too slow!
The flowers are laughing, they tickle my nose,
In this wacky wonderland, I'll gladly compose.

So grab that small moment, let it twist in your hand,
Life's too full of laughter, let's make a new band.
We'll sing out our joys, let the whole world see,
How savoring seconds can set our hearts free.

Tapestry of Tiny Wonders

A journey on clouds, we're sailing in socks,
The floor is a trampoline, so jump and don't stop!
With a splash of confetti and a tickle from time,
The tiny goldfish grace us with bubbles that rhyme.

The moon plays hopscotch, jumping over our heads,
While ninjas do cartwheels right over our beds.
A slice of the sky drops a wink from above,
In this giggling tapestry, we find boundless love.

The spoons start to dance, just watch them all twirl,
As I tie all my dreams into one silly swirl.
A whirlwind of wonders, we giggle and twine,
In every small moment, a sparkle divine.

With laughter as music, we'll make every scene,
In this vibrant existence, we're silly and keen.
So grab little wonders, let's twirl without care,
In this delightful journey, there's joy everywhere.

Joys in the Ordinary

A sock with a story, it dances alone,
The toast with a face says, 'Please leave me scone!'
In every small moment, a chuckle will rise,
From the cats in pajamas, to all of our sighs.

With a wink from the fridge, it whispers, 'I'm cold,'
As leftovers plot world domination, I'm told.
The remote hides and seeks, like a kid on the run,
In this game of the mundane, I'm still having fun!

The kettle sings opera, it's warming my brew,
While the spoons are all gossiping in quite a stew.
A car horn goes beep-beep, what a curious sound,
In every small hiccup, laughter's always found.

So let's toast to the mishaps that color our days,
In the silly, the quirky, let's dance and get lost.
For joy isn't grand, it's in all that it brings,
In the ordinary moments, the heart laughs and sings.

Enchanted Threads of Existence

In socks that don't quite match their pairs,
A dance of mismatched flair declares.
The cat jumps high, a frenzied leap,
As laughter hides where secrets keep.

A ladle sings in pots and pans,
While flour fluffs like magic plans.
The dog wears socks, a goofy sight,
In kitchens where we laugh and bite.

A goldfish dreams of swimming far,
In a bowl that thinks it's a car.
The toaster pops like it's a show,
As breakfast crumbs take flight and go.

So here's to quirks and odd designs,
To silly jokes and tangled lines.
Each day's a treasure, funny and bright,
In the yarn of life, we weave delight.

Radiance in the Everyday

The sun turned up in awkward styles,
With pigeons strutting silly miles.
A squirrel steals a slice of pie,
As neighbors yell, 'That rascal's sly!'

Umbrellas bloom on sunny days,
While puddles dance in shiny ways.
A dog in shades, all cool and wise,
As we laugh at its silly guise.

The vacuum hums a jazzy tune,
While socks get lost like balloons in June.
The toaster's voice begins to chime,
As breakfast spills, it's slapstick time.

We twirl through life, both bold and shy,
With quirky tales that never die.
In every twist, a giggle sighs,
As laughter lingers, sweet surprise.

Moments That Sing

A spoon can spin a tale or two,
In kitchens where the heart renews.
The fridge hums softly in the night,
While leftovers take off in flight.

A cactus with a party hat,
Has guests that whisper, 'Just look at that!'
The goldfish throws confetti fun,
In bubbles echoing, 'We're not done!'

In the garden where weeds play hide,
A worm wears glasses with great pride.
The sunflowers wink with silly glee,
As bees buzz by, quite merrily.

So let your heart skip, leap, and spring,
For laughter's found in pretty things.
In every giggle, a melody rings,
With joy in moments that life brings.

Petals on the Breeze

A dandelion whispers a wish or two,
While kids chase it like they always do.
The wind plays tricks with every hat,
As giggles float, and one falls flat.

Butterflies wear polka-dot gowns,
While a cat in a crown just lounges around.
The daisies dance a funky jig,
As ants march by, a tiny brigade.

The sun slips down, a clumsy show,
While shadows stretch, and laughter flows.
A toddler spins, arms open wide,
As giggles burst, they can't abide.

So here we twirl on nature's stage,
With whimsy gently turning the page.
In these fleeting laughs, we find our ease,
Like petals swirling on a breeze.

www.ingramcontent.com/pod-product-compliance
Lightning Source LLC
Chambersburg PA
CBHW060126230426
43661CB00003B/352